Heart Abounding

Book 7 Reflections of God Moments
56 One Minute Devotionals

Journal

Heart Abounding
Book 7 Reflections of God Moments
copyright © 2024

Written by: Donesa Walker
Design by: Will Baten
Edited by: Kelley Inderman

The Surgeon's Tools!
Hebrews 4:12-13

What happens when we doubt His word?

Ever wonder why it seems like life is easy for others and hard for you? We all have troubles, what is it that determines how we endure the hard times?

Key thought for today:

Abounding While Abased!
Philippians 4:6-7, 12-13, 19

Abounding =

Abased =

Do others see Jesus in your words, actions and deeds?

When you are having a meltdown, who's your parent?

Key thought for today:

The Blessed Hope!
Revelation 1:7-8, 3:10-12, & 4:8, 11

What is the portal to glory and away from your problems?

What do you need to do to get into the atmosphere of praise?

Key thought for today:

Count It All Joy!
2 Corinthians 7:10

I prefer my own way, why would I choose to be directed by God's laws/instructions?

Being in the Master's way means He feeds me, clothes me, provides for me and directs my path. But does it mean I give up my perceived freedom to do what I want?

Key thought for today:

The Joy Stealers!
Micah 6:8

Fair =

So how do we make sure we are DOing what is right?

How do we have balance/alignment in our life?

What is our source of Joy?

Key thought for today:

Who's Your Papa?
Romans 8:1-2, 15-17

What would you do today if you knew that everything you asked would be granted and money was no object?

Now think, is that according to the will of God?

Are there highs/lows Joys and triumphs? You bet. Do things trouble us and make us question His goodness? Will you feel lonely and lost sometimes? Will you feel like God has failed you sometimes? Unfortunately, yes. Why?

Who's your daddy?

Key thought for today:

Full of Self and Soul Empty!
Habakkuk 2:2-4, 20

What is written on my walking billboard of life for others to read: From my FB to my actions? Do they read self-indulgence or self-sacrifice? Do they read worldly wealth or Heavenly wealth? Are they reading words of wisdom falling from the throne of grace or a quick fix solution of self-indulgence? What is my billboard of life advertising? Do they see Jesus in Me?

Key thought for today:

The Cozy Flame!
Nahum 1:7-10

Do you know how mighty Samson was when he was used by God?

How can I live in the place where God wants me?

What if I have become dry kindling used up by the world soaked in the kerosene of sin?

What will the pillar of fire be to you?

Key thought for today:

A Solid Foundation!
Matthew 7:24-27

What does God mean when He says to build our home's foundation in Him?

Key thought for today:

He Chose Me!
John 15:1-4, 16-17

What is the Root command He gives to us?

Key thought for today:

Making the Deal!
Mathew 6:14-15, 34

Trust =

He said if you refuse to do your part in the work of God in your life then He cannot do His. What is the key to resting in His promises?

Key thought for today:

Wonderful Words of Life!
Proverbs 18;4, 13, 15, 20-21

God uses the power of words to change lives. What are some ways that words can give life?

Where does the power of words lie?

Key thought for today:

Sheltered In The Arms of God!
Isaiah 41:11-13

Sheltered =

What does it mean to you to be sheltered by God?

Key thought for today:

The Knowing!
Proverbs 20:5, 15, 24, 27

How do we gain the understanding and "knowing" that God wants us to have?

Key thought for today:

The Good, The Proud and The Humble!
James 4:2-6, 16-17

So if our sin nature is so strong, how do we live a life reflecting God's love?

Key thought for today:

Putting Out Your Best!
Colossians 4:5-6

What is it about us that reserves the best for a day that never comes, failing to realize that time has passed and the best reality has happened while you were waiting?

How are you using your words?

Key thought for today:

It's Elementary My Dear...!
Matthew 18:2-5, 10

What is the element that unlocks the power of God's love and activates His heart actions?

Key thought for today:

GPS (God Positioning System)!
John 14:5-7, 9-10

If God is your "GPS", how do you rely on Him?

What is it that turns you around?

Key thought for today:

God of Hope Who Conquers Fear!
John 20:20-21, 29-31

How do we conquer fear in our life?

Are you walking in the cloud of miracles and failing to do what it takes to activate them in your life and the lives of others? Are you walking in inactivated faith because you are allowing doubt/fear to cloud your mind? Are you simply going passively through the motions of life never realizing that your faith must arise to activate the Eternal Hope?
How can you activate the Holy Spirit in your life today?

Key thought for today:

Bankrupt Without Love!
1 Corinthians 13:3-7

How have you invested your love in those around you?

Key thought for today:

In His Presence...Filled with His Purpose!
James 4:1-10 & Ephesians 6:10-18

How do we remain steadfast in His presence?

How do we know what His purpose for us is?

Key thought for today:

Something Beautiful!
1 Timothy 2:1-3, 8-10

Who and what are you praying for today?

Allow some time today to focus in prayer on these needs.

Key thought for today:

Resilience or Reliance!
Romans 8:5-8, 18-21, 29-30

Are you anchored in Him, rooted in Him, ready to
allow the resiliency to be Faith in Him rather than self?

Key thought for today:

Open Up, Quiet Down and Wait Passionately!
Psalms 37:5-7, 18-19, 34

Is it difficult for you to sit and wait quietly or does it come easily for you? Why?

What have you discovered when you sit and wait on Him?

Key thought for today:

Infertility!
Isaiah 54:1-6, 11-17

What is the promise given here?

How are we to prepare?

Key thought for today:

The Don'ts That Equal the DO!
Romans 13:8-10

Fear + God's Love =

Sum up in your words what it means to be fruitful in love.

Key thought for today:

Time Is Not on My Side!
2 Peter 3:8-9

Have you ever experienced a "Holy Moment"? What happened?

Are you leaving space and time for God to use you?

Key thought for today:

The Fraud!
Jeremiah 3:22-25

How have we been deceived by false doctrines and where has that gotten us?

What must we do to get back into the safety of God's arms?

Key thought for today:

Bless God!
Psalms 103:19-22

A blessing is:

What was the supreme blessing of all mankind?

What will you do with this supreme gift of Blessing?

Key thought for today:

Written in Red!
Isaiah 1:18-20

Do you have any other representations of red that are significant to you?

What about a particular scripture?

.

Key thought for today:

Heart Swell!
Isaiah 60:1-7

Are you waking up to each new day embracing the coming of Christ's return? What are some things that are happening that tell you this day is coming soon?

Key thought for today:

The Naked Truth!
John 14:1-4, 15-17, 21

What changes in your life could/should you be making today?

Are you walking in the Spirit of Truth or have you been blinded by the lies and deceit of this world? Ask The Holy Spirit to open your eyes and help you to see the truth.

Key thought for today:

Supple Prayer!
Luke 6:26-30

What are the benefits of practicing daily prayer?

What are some things you can practice praying about today?

Key thought for today:

Rivers of Light!
James 1:16-18

What did He say about the gifts of heaven?

Take a minute to appreciate all the goodness God has provided for you and write down a few that really stand out to you.

Key thought for today:

Beauty Refracted!
Proverbs 17:3, 8, 17, 22, 27

What is the key to being a reflection of the creator?

What does the gift of the power of the Holy Spirit help us to see, if we will seek Him?

Key thought for today:

The Paradise Crown!
Psalms 103:1-5

What are the six blessings that are mentioned in these scriptures?

What one thing is required of us in order to retain the Paradise Crown?

Key thought for today:

Lifeline of Promise!
Hebrews 6:13-18

Why do we let our own situations overwhelm us until we reach out to our earthly lifelines in despair rather than claiming and walking in His promises?

Do you have a promise that God has given you to stand on? Write it here and say it over and over. Apply the Word of God and hang on!

Key thought for today:

Joyful Recharge!

Psalms 119:1-7

Are you staying plugged in or do you need a recharge? Jot down a few things that you feel are draining your battery and go to God with them.

Key thought for today:

God Quest!
Psalms 24:1-6

Who can climb the Holy North Face of Mount God?

What is their reward?

Key thought for today:

Just Desserts!
Psalms 9:1-2, 7-10

What portion of God and His word are you seeking?

Are you diving into His word with gladness?

Key thought for today:

Free Life!
Galatians 6:14-16

Are you walking in a real relationship with Him where you have given Him all of you? Are you willing to lay down your own hopes, dreams and future to follow His?

What freedom is attained when you walk with Him?

Key thought for today:

The Blessing!
Numbers 6:24-27

Are you struggling or doubting that God wants to give you blessings?
Take some time to sit in His embrace and allow Him to "Hug" on you.

Speak words of blessing over yourself and others in your life today!

Key thought for today:

Bought Back!

Isaiah 41:5-7, 14-16

Are you feeling worthless and forgotten? Be encouraged and strengthened by His word. He has bought you with a price and He will never forsake you. Let God restore you, transforming you from nothingness to a useful tool in the kingdom of God.

Key thought for today:

Firm Foundation!
Hebrews 11:1-3

Where is your Faith level?

Do you believe that He is/will be a firm foundation?

Key thought for today:

Heart of Harvest!
Matthew 9:27-31, 35-38

Are you harvesting in faith believing or are you one of those who will miss the feast because you are too busy with your own agenda in this temporal realm?

What are you offering to those in need around you?

Key thought for today:

Forgiveness Habit!
Psalms 130:1-8

Is forgiving complete without the mercy of forgetting?

Are you able to move beyond the wrong into a place of true repentance and forgiveness?

Can we draw closer to the Source of love so much that His forgiveness and mercy become our lifestyle?

Key thought for today:

Fortunate Future!
1 Peter 1:3-5

What does it mean to put your all in Him?

What do you desire for your future?

Key thought for today:

Extravagant Dimensions!
Ephesians 3:14-21

What does the resurrection power of Jesus mean to you?

How can we experience the depth of His Love?

Key thought for today:

Consecrated Oneness!
John 17:13-19, 20-23

How can we experience complete joy?

Consecrated oneness with Christ is....

Key thought for today:

Stop, Drop and Listen!
Psalms 95:1-7

What is the key to opening the windows of heaven?

Have you gotten sidetracked by all the busyness of life? SDL!

Key thought for today:

Do You See It Now?
Deuteronomy 32:1-7, 39-43

Do you see that God is the one? List some ways that He has been there for you.

Spend some time thanking and worshiping Him.

Key thought for today:

Indispensable Weapons!
Ephesians 6:13-18

What are the weapons we are to use in order to stay steadfast when our battles are the strongest?

How is each one used?

Key thought for today:

God Steeped!
Matthew 6:30-33

Why does God allow the crushing and the pressing, the roasting and the steeping?

Shut in with Him and allow His fragrance to envelop your life.

Key thought for today:

Mature Joy!
John 15:11-15

What is mature joy?

J -

O -

Y -

Key thought for today:

Conceived In Love!
Matthew 7:7-11

Why do we believe that God is a trader of favors rather than a doting parent?

How should we approach Him when we have a request?

Key thought for today:

Deep and Steady Life!
1 John 4:13-16

How do people know we are sincere and passionate?

Are you walking a deep and steady life? Let His life breathe in and through you today.

Key thought for today: